Why I Write

WHY I WRITE

POETRY AND PROSE
BY
BARBARA GRIPPE

Published
by
French Creek Books
an imprint of

Cambridge Springs Press

Cover design by Franklin Grippe

ISBN 0-9717205-4-1

French Creek Books
Cambridge Springs Press
Box 105
Venango, PA 16440
www.cambridgespringspress.com

The names of some characters and places in this book have been changed to protect anonymity.

Contents

There is an appointed time for everything…a time to be born, and a time to die…a time to weep, and a time to laugh, a time to mourn, and a time to dance…

Ecclesiastes 3:1-4

Let me dwell in your tent forever
And hide in the shelter of your wings.

Psalm 61

We are going to be judged on love: not on how much we have done, but how much love we put into the doing.

Mother Teresa

WHY I WRITE

My parents have been my inspiration. I grew up in a loving Czech family. Writers grow with nurturing. My parents read to me. I went on to develop a passion for books and writing. I began to write a secret diary replete with lock and key. Today my journals are open. Practiced reading and writing habits are embedded within me.

Extraordinary seeds of thought took shape within my mother's kitchen. I was a curious apprentice. I would watch mom knead her bread dough in order to smooth out unwanted air bubbles. I applied mom's breadmaking lessons to my writing. I began to edit in order to clear my work of excesses. I wanted to strive for a smooth manuscript, preparing for the rising and the baking of each word and paragraph.

Outside the kitchen I was inspired by notable authors. Some of these artists gave me reasons to consider savoring words. I became a word detective, continued to seek premium words in order to have the finest ingredients while preparing my homebaked creations.

Today I place the dough into my literary oven with the same care and attention that I observed in mom's kitchen. I recall rising dough. I remember to cover loaves against damaging drafts. I place my work upon racks to cool. I continue to consider the next batch of potential ingredients. My youth was filled with the nourishment that produced my writing life.

I keep the oven warm.

RASPBERRY REFLECTIONS

Raspberry wine from Montreal
Recalled raspberries at our old house
When Dad plopped plump berries into white enamel pots
Rinsing radiant red morsels
Crushed ripened berries carefully poured into
Wood barrels in the basement far from mom's kitchen
Where in wintertime she simmered soup
Kneading wheat bread in early morning sunlight
Radio turned low yet loud enough to muffle other noises.
Familiar morning sounds with kitchen fragrances
Wafting into registers that stretched like steel fingers into
Second floor bedrooms where we would stir
Scramble to watch her punch dough down
Like a prizefighter
Loaves placed into oven
Later lavishly smothered with creamy butter
Served with abundant soup thick with vegetables
Beef clunking in broth.
A celebratory dinner when we would toast with
Dad's raspberry wine made the year before
One of those surprises
Always better than expected

My brother walked with me yesterday
In front of our old house
The berry bushes
Were choked by tangled weeds.

CROSSROADS

Mary, my mother, in her eighties
Works every day exercising her mind
Submerged in her crossword puzzles
Mary wears out dictionaries faster than shoes.

She tells me what to do
I say I need to keep my brain active
She repeatedly suggests crosswords
I say I need to look up meanings.

Her favorite is the *Pittsburgh Post Gazette*
She adds the *New York Times* on Sunday
Her eyes sparkle as she works to finish
Ready for each day's delivery.

I say she has developed an obsession
She says she is stretching her mind
She says when I cross over to retirement
I should start doing crosswords.

Mary has an active mind
She amazes me with her recall
She says she owes all to her puzzling
Maybe I should consider crosswords?

LILAC LANE

Dad sits in his lazy chair
Rocking back and forth during his day
With child-like expressions
Mixed with moments of confusion.

Mom prefers her straight-back bouncer
Looking at Dad when he is not looking
In her direction, when they sit together
On their front porch (perch).

They sit, wait
Watch people walk by, wave,
While her hands gnarled with arthritis
Match his hands, shaky, uncertain.

They live on Lilac Lane
With fall flowers still blooming
On both sides of the house.
Flowers always flowers.

Where Mary and John
Seem less and less
like they used to be
And more and more
Like tired, weary travelers.

DAD

We went to my first Van Gogh show at the Carnegie
Fine-penciled drawings.   I was eight.
I asked, "Are these real?"
Again I asked, "Are these real?"
"Yup," he said. "This is the real thing."

Dad taught me to drive on bumpy roads that would
soon be smooth
Sometimes   bumps got in the way
Slamming brake and clutch   out of gear   the car stalled
He never had patience

Drove me to the high school dances
Picked me up afterwards
Would not allow me to go in cars with friends

He took me to Westinghouse where he worked
His cubicle looked small but neat
He never said much yet loved to
Surprise   float a wry sense of humor

Now when I walk into the house
I feel like a visiting nurse

Sometimes he seems to know me.

RIGMAROLES

Twirling

Whirling   Whirling

I began to unwind ropes of the swing attached to
        sturdy oak boughs.
Practicing, I twisted the swing as tight as a wet,
        soppy scrubbing mop.
Releasing my grip, I spun out into dizzying jerks,
        easing into eventual gentle swishing.

Dad walked by and said, "Why don't you take it easy?
        You don't need to keep going the way you do."
Trying topsy-turvy movements, I went reeling through
        swelled pockets of hot air surrounding me.
Summers were slowly stagnant without windy
        wintertime spasms.

Dad said, "You get into too many rigmaroles
        That seem to go on and on without stopping."
He never told me what he meant
        Or what he thought.

The swing began to wind down as I turned in his direction.

Stooping to squeeze the warm wood of the
         wheelbarrow handles,
         he started to move away from me.
His veined sunburnt hands were shaking,
Looking skyward, I settled back into my wind-ups
         Without pausing.

Whirling

Twirling   Twirling

THE PARADE:
Memorial Day, May 28, 2001, Yardley, PA.

I.
A painter creates at easel with pigment along the
periphery of Afton Lake. I write with pen and notebook,
paint with words, absorb the ambiance of the day. The
artist and the writer walk toward the center of town.
Cameras catch candid moments.

II.
Under partly cloudy skies streaked with some sunshine,
people move purposely to find places along Main Street.
Men, women, and children of all ages wave the
American flag, some carry folded chairs. Others sit on
the curb of the street, some with coffee cups or water
bottles. We honor those who have served our country in
combat.

III.
Pearl Harbor was bombed December 7, 1941, the day
Uncle Ray and 2,400 others were killed in less than two
hours.

IV

When I was studying American history in grade school my mother told me about Uncle Ray. She showed me his picture. He stood tall and handsome in his uniform with his arm around Aunt Margaret in Pearl Harbor. My grandmother said the Army sent my aunt his Purple Heart. I had no idea what that meant. My aunt remarried. When she died my cousins got to keep the medals and letters. That was a long time ago. I did not understand the words World War. Over the years I have held a firm conviction that we do not have the right to kill others at any time during our short lives. I wish I could have met my Uncle Ray. His picture shows him to be a kind man with a gentle smile.

24

GROWING OLDER

"…Loving beings are no longer other. They are a part of you, and you share in their joys and tribulations…"   Czeslaw Milosz

As you grow older
You find yourself going
To more and more
Memorial services
Visiting more friends
In the hospital
Taking friends for
Treatments
Therapy for worn ligaments
Muscles or lack of
Driving more often to
Deliver meals on wheels
To those who do not have
Their former transportation
In doing so you are aware
Others will be doing the same
For you
All too soon
We know
It has everything to do
With being no longer other

BROKEN HEART

When memory gets in the way (watch out)
Your can find yourself unable to
Begin each day in reality where
You are surrounded by (living) people
Who hold you, hug you, leaving imprints
Upon your innermost thoughts like an
Ink stamp that leaves an indelible impression
Guarding against living inside past memories
Something you could easily slip into
Without tugging from a real world
Telling truth before turning to maudlin
Avoidance inability to accept loss like
People whose daily ritual
At cemetery plot standing at
Headstone fluffing up plastic flowers
Dusting off tombstone
Reminders of grandma
Dying months after her spouse
Not willing to go on (alone)
Without him.

REFLECTIONS

"Analects " Confucious

At birth I was a free-floating spirit.

At one I was ready to speak.

At two I was ready to walk.

At sixteen I was ready to dance.

At twenty-five I was ready to find my first job.

At thirty-two I was ready to marry.

At forty-four I was ready to raise a family.

At fifty-six I was ready to face a divorce.

At sixty-three I was ready to learn more of life's lessons.

At seventy I was ready to embrace new friendships.

At eighty-eight I was ready to love my life.

At ninety-one I was at peace with my world.

At one hundred I was a free-floating spirit once again.

EASTER DINNER

White lace hand-woven tablecloth
    starched, stretched,
Dyed eggs, freshly cut flowers,
    add springtime tint, tone.
Platters prepared, savory ham
    bakes, bubbles, sizzles in oven,
Peppery polish sausage wafting,
    relish, vegetable trays filled.

We arrive, husbands, wives, offspring,
    arms outstretch, enfold, embrace,
Familiar cherished rituals
    continue when we come together.
All take momentary views,
    parents presiding at each end of our circle,
Their love takes us to earlier times,
    connected at our crowded chrome table.

ELIZABETH

Her name reminds me of Shakespearean times, the theatre, women who wore long gowns with tight waistbands, Romeo and Juliet sonnets, young girls who sat by a stained glass window doing fine needlepoint under supervision of an elderly aunt or relative, living in drafty castle rooms with only fireplaces to keep warm in wintertime, long, lonely, dark hallways that chilled them to the bone, even in summer months. I envision Elizabeth being bright, witty, a skilled vocalist, humming popular tunes of the day as she captures the attention and devotion of each member of her family. Now Elizabeth has our heartfelt love as she smiles and coos, learning to walk, making small talk, and taking our hand and getting to know her grandmothers, aunts, uncles, and each person who adores her every minute they are in her company. Elizabeth could grow up to be in a Shakespearean acting company or she could become a prominent vocalist or an opera diva. She can explore each year, become aware of many career choices. But I shall always see Elizabeth as the queen of her castle, just as she is now in this the second year of her life. Lovely Elizabeth Heather, my granddaughter.

PANIC AND A PENNSYLVANIA POET

The town of Panic is located north of Punxsutawney. As an aspiring poet I had plans to spend some time in the adjoining town of Desire. These two Pennsylvania towns were separated by farmland, trees, and a narrow road. Odd place names have always drawn my interest and since nearby DuBois is not a great distance from my home, I decided to drive to the area. I planned to stop in the local libraries and read more about the history. In the early 1800s the first European settlers were Germans and Scotch-Irish farmers. I could envision the early settlers as I read accounts from that time period. Somehow I knew there was a poem to be found.

I was gravitating towards Desire with a pure romantic purpose. I ended up in Panic because it was the first town I reached after the eight-mile drive from Punxsutawney. I wasn't surprised the media never mentioned Panic when they were televising for Groundhog Day. As I opened my car door, I realized why the media never gave this town a second blink. There was nothing there to shoot for a television audience, especially in the wintertime.

Panic is quiet and unassuming. There are no auspicious buildings, there's just a lot of space. There are a few farms but the most you can gather after panning a telescopic lens is a wide, wide yawn.

After getting out of my car and stretching my legs, I knew that the serenity and singular peacefulness in this quiet town was producing a calmness of spirit that I could cherish, particularly through my poetry. I opened my notebook after I found a fairly solid rock to perch myself upon. I began my note-taking that quicklydeveloped into several short narrative poems. Normally this process takes me several hours and sometimes days. Here in Panic time seemed to flow from my heart into my fingertips, easing gently onto the computer screen.

Looking up into the clear azure sky above me, I moved my eyes and experienced easy-going peaceful thoughts far removed from any resemblance to panic. I had anticipated finding this calm joy in Desire, but to my surprise I had found the best place to be. Joanne, a friend, said that some of the best gifts we can find are those we had never thought about or anticipated. I had never planned to reach such a spot in such a short space of time.

Panic and poetry can work without a departure to desire.

ULTRA VIOLET

(after a celebration in New York prior to the opening of the Andy
Warhol Museum in Pittsburgh)

Isabella was her real name
wearing navy catsuit
with magenta boa
draped flamboyantly over shoulders
never revealing any clues of her past fifty-eight years
about appearances in Andy's films
despite her illness
after being bedridden many months
beginning her spiritual studies
painting angels
because it is a "time of communication"
angels are messengers
mixing angels with airplanes
believing technology
should be guided by morality.
She had a prophetic dream
about Andy wanting
to take things with him.
She told him:
"the Shroud has no pockets."

WINTERTIME WINDOW

My keyboard faces
Wide windows where
Snowflakes fall in steady assault upon
Pine trees and meandering roads
Interrupting my thoughts about
What to do
Making it impossible to
Pick up pieces that keep
Wandering in my mind
When I went up the stairs
Began my writing day
Before snowy hypnosis
Dreaming of that day
When we walked along
The Seine with heavy
Scent of fragrant lilac
Making us dizzy
Eager to meet others at
Our outdoor cafe
Sipping Beaujolais

Flirting with a
French man wearing
His snug beret with
Coffee eyes
Come hither looks
Beckoning and becoming

How can I write when
These sensual mind movies
Continue to interrupt
With determination I close the computer
Walk with a bounce down each step
Pour a glass of Beaujolais
Continue my French freefall.
Love what happens when
I let go
Look out the window
On a cold snowy day.

UNDER THE OAK TREE
Marblehead, Massachusetts

Rhythms of my morning ritual
Begin under the rugged tree
Gliding gulls above sailboats within the wide
Landscape painting set before me
On the bench atop former fort barriers
The ocean moans gently
Readily splashing its jazz
Against jaggy rock shaped sites
Miles of boulders looming large
Fronting fishermen's homes at
Harbor's edge.

Inhaling fresh fishy air
For me these fumes are far
Better than purest air
Abundant Marblehead essence provides
Energy when we weave our way
Along narrow one way
Olde Town streets.

Until we see the sign
Above "Much Ado"
Creaking wooden floorboards
Eke old-fashioned odors
While editions of
Out of print volumes
Beckon to be opened.

THE RAM
in the Sculpture Garden, Marblehead, Massachusetts

He stands stiff, erect, looking forward
Horns almost intermingled
With chunky bits of brass
That appear to be
Part of his hide,
Never moving when
Bees sting,
His edges turning green,
A sign of aging in the sun,
No doubt.

SCOTT AND ZELDA

Yellow haired lavender eyed Princetonian
Walking with deliberate swagger
Suggesting he could almost fly.
Genius writer at her side.

Zelda breathless
Much the way
Your penetrating eyes
Pierced my own breath.

Sealed with solid smiles
You stifled my breathing yet
Your presence provided essence
Genius writer no longer at my side.

In the middle of summer
After intervening lambent afternoons
My mind absorbed freedom
Far from our bittersweet dark days.

THE EAVESDROPPER

What you heard recently is true. While in their house I heard her whisper softly to the tall, dark, distinguished man in the navy pin-striped suit. I could see that he had deep, penetrating bluish-green eyes that responded immediately when they continued their private almost inaudible conversation. I did manage to catch her last few words as she prepared to walk over to the other end of the room. She said: "In a few minutes, after the photo session."

Hired as an assistant for the photo shoot, I arrived early enough to give me time to look around. This particular gig was a part of the symphony benefit project. The cocktail party was preliminary to the informal meeting of the Board of Directors.

Assuming the air and posture of the bartenders I stood at the periphery of the large foyer. Slowly and deliberately I made my way along the side of the room to the alcove with the two chairs and the sets of floodlights. The woman walked briskly. She slowed down when she reached the green velvet chairs. She was twisting her gold wedding band with short, snappy movements. Her husband began nervously shuffling in order to position himself alongside her. You could tell he liked these public photo sessions, with people walking around sipping on their drinks, an audience yet not an audience. A few would stop and nod, not in direct approval, but in a casual manner of recognition.

He attempted to display perfection, while at the same time he had a harshness that was distracting. He had been the conductor of the symphony for the past decade and had never fully departed from his tight torso posture. That's what one of the passersby was telling her friend when I edged closer to the alcove.

As I approached, the conductor never once glanced at his wife directly. She was seated and attractively attired in a blue lapis velvet evening dress. Her soft and natural blond curls complemented the sure and even lines of her confident posture. Her poised hands were placed delicately in front of her. She smiled with a practiced schoolgirl grin, yet from my corner I could see her focus was stretched to the opposite end of the room.

Her husband, as I zoomed in for a closer inspection, appeared arrogant and agitated, suggesting he was seeking more attention. He had dingy, dull, brown hair. Streaks of gray were accented with a prominent bald spot in the center of his not too perfect tilted head. He was noticeably large, looming over his wife with breathing that rumbled like an old motor. Despite his formal dress there was an irritating aura of displeasure surrounding him. He had jerky movements of his hands that gave evidence of impatience as the photographer signaled and I adjusted the lighting. He never smiled, rather he twisted his mouth up and around as if he was chewing his tongue. Not a good situation for a publicity photo and I was tempted to tell him. I hesitated, fearful he would chew me out. His mouth did not seem friendly.

Not wanting to be the focus of his irritability, I looked the other way.

After the photo shot ended, no one seemed to notice when she methodically made her way down the side hallway. They never noticed as she slipped into the shiny jet-black sports coupe, nor did they see the car turn to the right, leading straight out of town.

WOMEN OF TEGUCIGALPA

Buses, bright turquoise, purple, bluegreen,
Calla lilies common as daisies on the left, right
Arcane architecture spanning four centuries,
No railroads,
Almost no airports.

Low concrete buildings,
Walls glisten glittery pink, dazzling yellow,
Pig's feet served as street food,
Hand-washed shirts sear on rocks,
Women, baskets on their heads.

Resolute, robust women,
So much weight pressing down, squeezing
Burning sensations pulsate with firmness,
Loads wobble, hands harden, knuckles crack.

With lively movements, their grasp clings to what they know,
Their eyes find what they are looking for,
Seek the children beyond their horizon,
They smile, sway their hips.

OUR WORDS

…Words strain
Crack and sometimes
Break under the burden
Under the tension, slip, slide, perish…
                                    —T.S.Eliot

Words can crush   pierce   pulverize
Grind someone we love into
Sandy bits that blow into the wind
Never to be recovered   retrieved   repaired

Words can induce horror beyond description
When uttered with vengeance   hatred   scorn
Ill-fated pronouncements   placed   upon
People   who will never   learn the lessons.

Words can also lift us higher than clouds
Words can encircle those we love with truth
Our words can give reassurance   beyond   basic
Gifts of words can hold meaning   secure

Those who are reaching   eyes begging
Seekers of strength   beyond   borders
Not for one   rather several   loved   ones
Who may never learn the lesson.

THE WINDOW

What is so serene
As when an older woman leans
To see a hummingbird
Through her tiny bedroom window.
She begins to focus upon
Trumpet vines that tremble
While stormy breezes
Bring shackled rhythm.
Was she a gardener?
A poet?
Already
Her mind fades,
This window
Her final view.

THE AIRPORT

Women in business suits
Never notice children crying
Nor mothers who wipe their tears.
Men with briefcases
Pull light luggage
Several carry computers
Seniors sit in golf carts
Drifters make their way
Shopkeepers open gates
Brewed coffee tempts
Late passengers
Half-running with
Departure announcements
Airline personnel make haste
Relatives await arrivals

Anxious to depart
Give our ticket
Glide past security
Never detected
Heavy heart
Lighter now
Looking forward
We proceed
Our footsteps firm
Straightaway
Without threat or
Fear of reprisal
Only the promise of
A new life
Or so we thought.

BARBIE'S PARTY

Turning forty did not unsettle
Her since it was similar to
A decade ago when
She marked each
Year with notes
In her journal
Reminders of
Changes in her clothes
Hemlines dropped
Hair color highlights
Knowing she would
Have a party
At seventy
With or without ken
Never admitting to
Cellulite cover-ups.

A TALL TALE

Kenny Shoulder had to stand on a stool in order to kiss her under the mistletoe in eighth grade. The school bus was late, giving a couple of the boys time to throw this thing together, a surprise for an unsuspecting tall girl.
It was her first kiss.

This is the story of how a tall woman, a writer, finally answered a question but did not fully realize she answered the question until she finally wrote the story. The key word is finally. The writer in question does not like to finish stories in a final way. Instead she, the writer, loves to leave things open for editing and changes, otherwise known as an unfinished piece of work. The writer admittedly has many first chapters and only a few final drafts. That's her true prose assessment. She was happy her poetry publication had not been on that same slow production track.
In an effort to make a significant prosaic leap of faith the writer took herself by the shoulders and gave herself a few proverbial shakes and said silently: " For Pete's sake, snap out of it." After feeling quite good about the self-discipline she was thrusting upon herself, she gave herself a treat: a glass of wine while reading the recent *New Yorker* delivered that day.
The piece that became pivotal for her was an essay about a woman living near Taos Mountain, a ninety-year-old Saskatchewan-born Abstract Expressionist painter. Agnes Martin has been the recipient of many awards including the National Medal of Arts. Her paintings now sell for millions and she was quoted as saying, "I spend a lot of time just sitting, painting in my head." Agnes said first, painting is hard work and secondly "I'm always

painting in my imagination." That hit a chord of inspiration for the writer. Hmmm. Imagination, painting, writing.

Furthermore Agnes Martin said, "The happiest part of making paintings is when they go out the door and into the world." Another chord of recognition hit the writer. As a poet, the writer loved the fact that her poems were published and actually "out in the world." That was the happy part of making poems. Hmmm, like wood burning in a fireplace, the writer was getting into this train of thought. Some ideas were brewing in her mind. Hmmm." This is good," and she continued reading about Agnes Martin. A few days later, there was another conversation with a close friend and editor, Marcie.

The writer pondered: "It's awesome how these things, these seemingly unrelated incidents begin to intertwine and intersect in the most unanticipated direction. I wonder where this is going?" She decided to let it flow, let it go, not get anxious. It's easy to get uptight after talking to Marcie, the writer continued to fret silently. Marcie was editing some of the writer's latest poems; she pointed out some necessary corrections and suggested changes. One of the reasons Marcie was an excellent editor was a result of her honest, sometimes brutal and forthright manner. That's what was good. There was no sugar coating with Marcie. She told it as it was. Deep down in her inner core the writer wanted truth yet there were times when she did not want to go that way. It was a point of conflict between the two women, yet not an outright breach of friendship.

Part of the personality clash with Marcie had to do with the fact that she was a practicing psychologist, knowledgeable and keen, yet also a source of irritation to the writer.

Marcie had such a powerful presence she sometimes knowingly and sometimes not, would move into her professional clinical mode. If one wanted to see a shrink one had the option to do so. In the case of Marcie, if you wanted her professional opinion she would give her pronouncements and suggestions. The downside of being friends with a psychologist, in the writer's opinion, is that sometimes the shrink creeps out and stretches its tentacles during some uninvited times. The writer does not want shrink time unless she asks for it. By contrast Marcie does not always abide with the writer's psychological misgivings, saying, "You can simply consider the suggestion."

On the particular day of their conversation and editing, Marcie, as is typical of her psychological-surprise technique, blurted out the following question: "Did you ever think about why you have had so many relationships with short men?"

"There she goes again," the writer mused to herself, jerking her head, giving Marcie that "don't go there" glance. Fortunately for the writer the telephone rang at that moment.

Marcie said she had to hurry to an appointment with a client and was out the door in the blink of an eyelid. End of story? No, wait, there's more. The influence of Agnes Martin's words hovered over the writer. Agnes talked about Beethoven on CDs, particularly his Ninth. She said: "Beethoven is really ABOUT something. I never watch television…I have no radio…I listen to music."

Well, the writer did not watch the tube, yet she did listen to the local PBS affiliate, and she did listen to music. In fact her entire life from early childhood had been filled with her mother's music, mostly classical; the radio and classical phonodiscs were a part of her early childhood. She began to think about those early days in mom's kitchen, watching her punch down her bread dough, like a prize fighter, with precision and accuracy. Her mom never missed a beat. She kneaded her bread to the rhythm of whatever was playing on the radio at that time. Grandma would be busy beginning to get the round wooden table set up for noodle making. Her homemade egg noodles were a family favorite. The golden dough floated lazily in the chicken broth, like long and slender shoelaces. Grandma would dry the dough on broomsticks around the periphery of the kitchen. The noodles were like shaky beads one might see dangling in a movie featuring a fortune teller.

Which brings us to the next part of the story: an answer or what the writer thought could be part of the answer to Marcie's question.

Having had at least a few courses in undergraduate psychology, the writer knew we are all influenced by our childhood experiences, either indirectly or not so.

This brings us to her mom's kitchen, indirectly.

Imagine the scene: in grade school elderly Sister Agatha, secretly called Ag by some of the boys, had been promoting the eighth grade dance. The dance was the social high mark before graduation from St. Coleman's, prior to going on to either public junior high or to a Catholic prep school. After having boys pull hair, throw slimy spit balls or other gross insults, including having one's face "washed with snow" in the school playground in the winter, the girls were, well, not eager to warm up to the idea of the "Big" Dance.

There was another problem: many of the boys were short and most of them were shorter than the writer and her friend Jean Bush. The two girls were the tallest girls in the class. Their humiliating punishment was the placement by Sister

Ag at the end of all processions in church. Since students at St. Coleman's had many church functions to attend the two tall girls ended up marching together for eight years. There was a bonding between the two but it could never include dancing with one another, God Please, Never.

Sister suggested that boys and girls go home and ask their older brothers and sisters to help them with practicing for the dance. One shaky hand waved with a question: "What if we are the oldest and we don't have an older brother or sister, Sister?"

Agatha had a quick and easy answer: "Why, I'm sure your mother or father would help you. If they can't, come back tomorrow with a signed note from one of your parents (the school rule was a signed note for permission) saying you can stay after school for a practice session. We can settle this tomorrow, class dismissed."

The writer, always anxious with an overactive imagination, could envision the practice session: girls and boys lined up at opposite ends of the gym eyeing each other with equal amounts of misgiving and mistrust. She could hear Sister say: "find yourself a partner" and she imagined she saw Jean Bush standing in front of her. She went home upset, frustrated, a bundle of nerves.

When she arrived home her mother was busy getting the dinner plates out of the side cupboard. It was an hour before their evening meal. Things were hectic in the kitchen with grandma complaining because someone bumped one of the broomstick handles. Noodles were scattered around the floor. At this moment in time, the writer, tears in her eyes looked at her mother and said she needed help. She needed dance lessons; her eyes pleaded and begged for her mother's sympathy. Mary, her mother, was always a quick thinker, with three young children and a mother of her own always asking questions. Mary looked at her daughter, smiled, squeezed her hand tightly, then said, "I have the answer: you can do what I did when I was your age, you can dance with a broomstick. It's easy. Let me show you." She quickly whisked her daughter into the living room, grandma limping after them saying she could help. It all happened too fast. Before she knew it the daughter was dancing with a broomstick, awkwardly moving(step one, two, three....) to an old recording of Johnny Mercer's popular song of the 1940s:

> *Dream when the day is thru,*
> *Dream and they might come true,*
> *Things never are as bad as they seem,*
> *So Dream, Dream, Dream.*

If you learned to dance holding a short broomstick handle it would not be a stretch to think you could be comfortable dancing with a short partner. As it turned out Kenny Shoulder, shorter than the writer, was the boy she ended up dancing with at the "Big" eighth grade dance. He was taller than the broomstick handle, but not much. Jean Bush danced with Jimmy Braunger who was shorter than Kenny. Sister insisted that everyone change partners after each record (it was their very first sock hop) but of course no one did. They were stuck to each other like taffy. It would be too painful to try another dancing partner at this dance. Maybe, they would reconsider other dancing options IF there was a next time. There was a next time when they all went to public junior high school.

HEAVEN:
an earthbound vision reading the F. Scott Fitzgerald letters

Humans wonder
Ponder about Paradise
See all sorts of earth-like
Features both bars and scars
Fitzgerald at the Grand Ritz
Smiling along with fellow authors
They execute ethereal glances
Royal writers give to one another
After their prizes have been bestowed
Sometimes posthumously
Better later than never.

KISSING
after "Presumption" by F. Scott Fitzgerald

She soon reminds him,
"I've kissed too many people.
I'll have nothing left
If I keep kissing people."

He was bright enough
He understood her reference
After more movements of
Her fine delicate lips.

A poor yet spoiled boy
He was a stark contrast to
Culpepper Bay's best yet
He went on with his kissing.

MADRID TERROR

In Marrakech
Immoral men
Made their way into
Madrid metros
Their hands hoist
Prod pockets
They push then shove
Within sharp corners
My screams turn into
Screeches that create
Sharp chest pains while
Older women encircled
Chanting prayers
With Spanish firmness
We stumbled into the station
Our tears fell upon
Gran Via Boulevard.

NAMES OF TEA
after Nola Garrett*

All week by sheer potency you protected
my composure, giving calm and comfort as
I struggled with dark specters: shadows,
suggestions, shades of anxiety, anticipation, spinning within
deepest thoughts buried in another lifetime.
In March you granted relief with
oil of bergamot, soothing silly thoughts
that had no reality, giving solace, relief
from pressures built up long ago.
All summer sipping Chinese oolong, knowing
my psyche was refreshed, I could smile in
sunshine, in afternoon hammock respite.
Stretching my eyes to tops of
trees swaying from strong breezes
I heard each note sung by orioles
busy with sliced oranges on deck perch.
Tonight through pine trees sticky with
resin and ethereal ghosts you fled.

O Darjeeling, Orange Pekoe, English Breakfast, Earl Grey.

*See Garrett's "Names of Curtains"

ODE TO A DEAD SPOUSE

Ashes in marbled urn
On the corner of
Cold stone mantle
Photos atop television
Always staring
More and more photos
On frigid (metal)
Refrigerator door
Several more photos
On your chest (of drawers)
Dark solemn eyes
Look for something
I close your front door
Leave behind a heavy
House shrine.

TRUTH

One thing I learned (by experience)
Over the years is not to tell the
Truth to those we care about.
That is the last thing they want to
Hear from someone they trust.
They reject verbal vitamins,
Rather they savor
Thoughts of the taste of honey in
Cake baked in their honor (to
Celebrate their birthday).
What I remember was someone saying,
"What can I say?"
Which meant she could not say
That the thing about truth is
You want it and you don't want it
But when you get it
You can never erase it
Etched onto your brain

GENERATIONS OF MUSIC

For as long as I can remember Art and Music have offered me a haven and respite from the mundane aspects of daily living. From a very young age, pre-school and beyond, we would wake to the sound of classical music playing softly in mother's kitchen. Our family had hot oatmeal breakfasts in the wintertime because mom said it was a good way to warm up before going out to wait for the school bus. Her other gift was to have soothing music as a way to keep us unrushed before we dashed outside, busy for the rest of the day. The music had a calming affect that was almost magical. Our mother's smile, her cooked cereal and her music gave us a good jump-start, a subtle way of saying, "You will have a good day."

Over the years appreciation for music in our life developed and changed in the best possible ways. In high school we loved what is now called Fabulous Fifties music. Our school dances featured The Platters singing "Only You," The Vogues with "Turn Around, Look at Me," and many others. The music is still fun to listen to and often we play a few of the oldies but goodies, fondly recalling school friends and the memorable times we shared. As we progressed through our college years we settled into classical music, influenced by music professors and friends. We integrated our new appreciation for abstract art along with our continued love of classical music. After we were married and had sons of our own we in turn cooked hot cereal on cold winter mornings along with the classical music offered on PBS.

Recently I visited my son and family in South Carolina. I was delighted to find that the same gifts of classical music are now being offered to our young grandchildren. Three generations of music, warmth, and love continue to inspire as we spend time with one another. My sons play classical music in their homes and in their vehicles. My parents were influential in a dramatic, inspiring fashion. I can give testimony to their gift of music and know it is evident.

The music is playing softly as I type.

MARCH 29

11:44 p.m., a dark night when I came into this world in Wilkinsburg, near Pittsburgh when Mary, my mother delivered her healthy baby girl, in the harshness of the maternity room lighting, with Dr. Roose telling her it was not unusual for the first delivery to take longer, new mothers not knowing what to expect, being unusually anxious, hold back the birthing process, and I did the same after twenty-three hours or more before giving birth to my first son who was no doubt as anxious to be born as his mother, when Mary became tense as I became tense in night-time labor pains that produce, sooner or later, the baby who had nothing to do with the timing, other than the natural inclination to be free from the bondage of the mother, free to breathe on his or her own, yet dependent upon the milk of the mother, knowing that the parents played the pivotal role from the second the sperm and egg collided, accidentally, since other sperm were there waiting for a egg, yet if you want me to make sense of this, you will have to wait while I speak of God's intervention, His pivotal role when I was formed in the womb, and why I pray for His direct intervention for Mary, to give her freedom, far from her earthly eighty-five years, because she is once again anxious, tense to the point of being back in the harsh lighting with our Dr. Roose at her side, only a senile husband who also wants his freedom to breathe without anxiety or being afraid to die.

BLONDE BOMBSHELL:
Turtle Creek memories

Some of us have heard the refrain, "She got her hair from a bottle," something the boys would chant in a smart alecky tone during our high school days. A few of my girlfriends experimented with new colors, mostly bleached blonde shades, in our junior year before the prom. Our blonde shades *were* from a bottle. We could not wait to try a new look.

We could care less about silly comments and criticisms. All of us had the firm conviction that blondes really did have more fun. Following an uphill battle with our mothers (mine said absolutely not) we entered the world of boys, blondes, and sex. We imagined we would turn into a sexy siren since some of the blonde senior girls were the most popular in our school. They were the ones dating the cutest seniors, waving to the rest of us after school. In our eyes they were the lucky girls going home in a cool convertible, with the top of the car rolled down, all the better to show off going down Main Street. We wore see-through scarves when riding in a convertible.

By stark contrast my immigrant grandmother wore a black babushka, the other end of the fashion spectrum. My mother said I would look cheap as a bleached blonde. My own hair at that time could best be described as dishwater blonde, not a good thing for an aspiring senior. My secret goal was to be in a convertible cruising Main Street after school, sitting very close to a secret love, a senior I had never talked to, only watched from a distance when he went to his locker. His name was Tim and he was a star basketball player, tall and handsome. My prom date was with an *almost* square friend that I had known since grade school. Ken was someone my parents approved of, yet I was sure my parents would love Tim once we started dating. It was only a matter of time and patience on my part. I would go to the prom with Ken but in the meantime I would continue to cruise through Eat n'Park with my girlfriends, looking for the opportunity to talk to Tim. That was my plan. I would bleach my hair lighter at my friend Janet's house, keeping my fingers crossed that my mother would not give me a drastic punishment. I decided to take my chances since my mind revolved around Tim and not around my mother's reprisals.

We took turns borrowing the family car and taking a few other girls. We told our parents we were going to the public library to return books, always a good excuse to borrow the car. We all pitched in to buy gasoline, then only about ten cents per girl. We would order small cherry Cokes. We would sip slowly, making our drink last for the entire evening.

The drive-in had trays that fit on the driver's side of the car. We would either visit friends in other cars or we looked out for the guys we were in love with, in my case tall Tim. He was on the skinny side, but he had the biggest smile at Turtle Creek High

MOM'S KITCHEN:
memories of my early Pittsburgh days

Whenever there's a pot of soup simmering in my kitchen I replay the many mental movies of Mom's kitchen. It is a reverie of choice to recall the cool, crisp autumn grade school days when we would walk into the warm embrace of our mother, maternal grandmother and their many edible gifts. My brothers and I hurried along Pennsylvania Avenue making our way towards the big white house. We lived east of Pittsburgh, in Monroeville. Mom always liked the fact that we lived on a famous avenue even though the houses on our street were modest and nondescript. All we cared about when we scurried from the school bus was what was cooking on the stove. My younger brothers raced to beat me to the long, encircling porch that wrapped around three quarters of our family home. We had many memorable times on the big porch, many family discussions and disagreements. My brother John claims he could smell the stuffed cabbages cooking blocks away. Sometimes we were served samplers, pieces of pie crust coated with butter, sugar and cinammon, leftovers from the three or four apple pies that were cooling on the sideboard. We waited for our dad to arrive since he had an avid appetite and would wink at us when we looked at him with our hungry expressions. We never had to wait an undue amount of time after setting the table, ready to dig in, something brother John said after the prayer before each meal.

NOTCH BABY

When my mother Mary talks about social security she never seems to have a smile, rather her countenance contorts in an unpleasant manner as she relates to me time and time again about the discrimination she has been forced to accept since what she refers to as "the powers that be" in the SS office will never fully admit or change rules in her favor or give refunds to those who were born in certain years, in her case 1918, punishing them for being born in a year that warrants a penalty, a lesser amount than others.

I never fully understood her ire and disdain until I learned the discriminatory practice continues. When I applied for social security, sadly it was apparent the notch baby attitude prevails for the year of my birth.

Now Mary and I sit, mother and daughter, consoling one another, knowing the system will continue to attempt to single out certain birth years as being unworthy of a full SS benefit, unless I begin to make some ripples writing and campaigning, making Mary smile since she knows it's an uphill battle but worthy of effort against a system bigger than small bands of notch babies.

FIRST BOOK

now it can be told after
years   months weeks
days hours   minutes
anticipation
trembling
recalling glimpses
memories of other times
falling
swaying
failing
fingering keyboard letters
hearing dissonant notes
like a piano
that needs tuning
revising   editing
themes indelibly etched
mindfully noted
preserved
paperbound
for all to read

FOR HERE AND NOW

Yesterday I smiled
Today I am somber.
Some days are like that.

Yesterday I was dancing
Today I am walking.
It's good to slow down.

The horizon I seek
Cannot be located.
Countless more exist.

I step in the stream,
But the water has moved on.
Sometimes things change.

IF I COULD CHOOSE

Some say it is better that a dear friend goes "quick"
With an "unexpected" heart failure, before he or she
Knows what happened, never knows if it hurts or not.
Who can know if a sudden exit is preferred, after all we
Do not have the option of saying what we want and where,
Since the decision is out of our hands, something we can
Never control even if we have been a controlling person
All of our lives, always making arrangements for everything
Making sure the things we want are executed exactly the
Way we want things to fall out in our preferred, orderly
Human style, the way we think we want things to work out
Even if we have made some mistakes along the way
We realize we are gaining wisdom, insight, we
Know how we would like to go from this earth
Not suffering an enduring ending with cancer as
Opposed to the fatal heart attack that could be like
Ripping off a stubborn-sticky bandage on an open wound
But what do we know about such things? Only what
We think we know but in truth do not know,

The price of being a control person is very high
When we will never learn the answer
Until after the fact. Still, my controlling self says
If I could choose it would be a gentle, slow senility.
If I could choose.

A.J.

He radiates superiority with almost every breath. Tells people what to do even if they don't want his advice. If you try to walk in the opposite direction, he will thunder over to your side. He'll point his finger to indicate direct disagreement. He can look straight into your eyes without hesitation. Once he gets going he won't stop. It's annoying. Much of what A.J. dishes out is disquieting because he will not take "No" for an answer. He can be like super glue when your skin starts to peel if you try to pull it.

My friends and I have known A.J. for years. A.J. stands for Anthony James although A could also stand for arrogance. We were colleagues at the same college. Our children grew up together. A.J. also had his widowed father living with him.

A.J. said his move to the hinterlands of Northwest Pennsylvania was a quirk of fate with the added incentive of a steady salary.

Short of stature, he has uneven, dark chestnut hair. That hair! It would flap from his forehead onto the tip of his nose. Then he would blow it aside with forceful breathing, similar to the air escaping from an inner tube. Holding his arms akimbo is yet another one of his typical stances. Those of us who know him can spot him blocks away. If you happen to catch a quick glimpse of him you might guess he is an easy-going personality. It's only when you get the second glance that you might begin to realize your perception of a gentle man turns out to be a shout-in-your-face kind of guy. No doubt about it, A.J. could be unpleasant, disconcerting and downright disagreeable. Sporadically there are times when A.J. undergoes an almost instantaneous turnaround. That's part of the puzzle.

A.J. often interferes with women, always trying to stop us in our tracks. Women are his prey. He loves to touch, pat, or otherwise make contact in an annoying way. Sometimes it's a squeeze on the arm or shoulder when you least expect it. He's a hands-on man in the true sense of the word. A.J. also has the energy of a tornado housed within his less than five-foot frame. He always appeared to be running down the hall in the Art building.

Without exception, A.J. was indifferent to suggestions. Within a short space of time he could exacerbate tense conditions whether he attended a general faculty meeting or a committee gathering. In contrast when he would convene to his studio, A.J. would settle into his creative mode. He's a furniture and wood artist who is forever fondling one of his works.

Despite his conflicting ways, some will say that A.J. did draw us into his kind sense of self. It did not happen overnight. Over the years he did mellow and he did change. One incident remains in my memory as a direct testimony. A few months before retirement, A.J. stopped by my office. He seemed to be troubled by something. He began to gaze beyond the glass window at the one end of the room. He was facing the maple trees that outlined the periphery of the campus. He said his dad died ten years ago to the day.

A.J. reached into his coat pocket. He pulled out some stones, said he was going to put them on his dad's gravestone. It was their family custom. The stones were the size of small peach pits. Two or three of the stones were fit snugly into the center of his palm. His hand was trembling. He glanced at me with watery eyes.

"My dad broke everything he touched," A.J. said in a quiet, hushed tone.

After a few moments he turned and walked away.

THE BREADMAKERS

It has been said bread baking, like the spirit of egalitarianism, is an activity of rising expectations. As in all things democratic, it is never that simple.

With many culinary challenges, I almost never experience complete powerlessness in the face of rising bread dough. Growing up in my mom's kitchen, I watched her breadmaking ritual with enthusiasm and eagerness tinged with a sense of sheer reverence and wonderment. I could hear the trapped air bubbles burst as Mom thrust her firm fist into the deep bread bowl she had placed upon what she referred to as her bread stool. She was short of stature yet she stood straight and upright, ready as she looked down into her doughland situated on the white enamel launching stool. She said she preferred standing in order to better survey her almost magical realm. This was before Maurice Sendak published his IN THE NIGHT KITCHEN. The sparkling white residue that covered this area of the kitchen captured me with a strong sense of reverence mixed with wonderment and equal measures of anticipation.

In my early school years I was included as part of mom's breadmaking ritual; it was intensely exciting. I would help add the flour, which in turn would coat everything with a soft, white powdery film. My breath floated into white puffs overhead, cloud-like and ethereal like thin sheets drying on our outdoors clothesline.

Mom and I would both wear her long, full-length aprons, the old-fashioned kind that cover both upper and lower torso. Despite this protection I still managed to get lots and lots of the white, what was to me, magic dust sprinkled over my arms, face, and hair. I resembled an indoor snow sculpture. I took satisfaction in the fact that the white look was an improvement over the brownish mud-pie look that I sometimes slipped into outdoors during the summertime.

Mom always advocated using bare, clean hands for our bread kneading. Currently she still maintains she is not interested in changing to a more modern bread-making machine. She says the joy of baking bread is directly related to knowing the exact feel and texture of properly prepared dough. Furthermore, she states there is a smooth elasticity that only comes from the constant, steady, push and pull of the hand and of the wrist. Mom holds one hand on the bread bowl keeping it firmly in position while a damp dishcloth underneath prevents the bowl from sliding.

Bread is the most ecumenical of foods because it offers the embodiment of home and hearth. Bread makes the house smell warm, cozy, and comfortable. Bread making with mom enabled both of us to relate to one another in many ways. We asked each other questions. Over the months and years we were able to learn more and more about one another, aspects that were positive and negative. Our bread making ritual kept us within an open communiqué that we could use to our best advantage. Many mornings my maternal grandmother joined us, giving the added level of another generation from which to glean and listen.

Years later I am convinced there is a place for family rituals involving parents, their sons and daughters, grandparents, other close relatives. I was fortunate to learn, for me, the wisdom and ways of a breadmaker.

STRAWBERRY WINDOW

STRAWBERRY WINDOW

We were walking in your neighborhood
The Upper East Side trattoria
Rich with simmering sauces   spiced with sausages
The section of the city   frequented by

Fast moving   people of all ages.
New York energy   was   a   propellant
Recharging us after a busy day
MOMA Midtown

Exhilarated   the chatter   never
Diminished   from the first cup of cappuccino
Always animated   everything
Fresh and frank   in Manhattan coffee shops.

Conversation spiked   at seven in the morning
The woman   next to our table   talking
To her friend   about her need to break up with
Her live-in   because he was getting too close to her.

In a blink of an eye   day was done
Dinnertime   stretching each step
Made our way   with   caution
Our rhythm and   movement restrained.

When we turn the corner   we   spot   strawberries
Bright and big as plums
Sweet and succulent   dripping with
Starchy white   heavy   whipped crème.

Crispy   crunchy   escarole salad
Hot crusty rolls   bottle of Bardolino
Hand cut   fettuccini noodles
Reminders of   our summers in Palermo.

Tables   squeezed together tight
Elbows   almost touching
We whisper   with heavy anxiety in our eyes
The   moment.

We related   the   moment
Turning the corner   after passing
St. Patricks   seeing the person
We did not want to see.

Attempting to   avoid   an
Almost   constrained   conversation
Boldly   rushing into the bookshop
Losing ourselves.

In a maze of shelves   we went
Around aisles   to remain
Hidden   temporarily
Crammed into the   bursting   checkout counter.

Never detected   safe   in a
City   conducive to
Anonymity and   seclusion
With crowds of   people cover.

After dinner we   slowly   savored
Crème laced lush   berries   know
We had achieved   our intended day
Devoid of   confrontation.

Unspoken sentiments
Linger like rain clouds   above our table
Perfunctory kisses   precede several
Pathetic   good bye embrances   shadowy
Slivers   in   the   strawberry window.

THE GATE AT THE GARDEN

Fair Quiet, have I found thee here?
And Innocence, thy sister dear?"
                Andrew Marvell, THE GARDEN

The gate at the
garden opens
beckons to her
eyelids stretch beyond
lacey iron gate
finds a path ringed by
thousands of fanciful tulips
she settles upon
teakwood bench
in search of surcease from dread
not able to know
to name what it is
is it fear of unknown horizons
is it beyond allees
wherein most often
women who know
confront branches
overheard amid
leprechaun sculptures
penetrate gnarled
crabapple canopies
wherein wintertime
storms she slides
stiffened boots scratch
permafrost pathways

considers empty branches.

NAMESAKE

Closing my eyes
I can see Grandma
squatting down on her
    bended knees
sowing seeds in
    her garden
never off balance
    steady serene smile
faded garden gloves
    falling apart
dress wrinkled
    splattered   tattered
taking time out from
    noodle-making
looking in my direction
her words echo
"Why don't you come
    over here
help me stand up
    careful
not to stand on my rows."

JOY:
April 5, 2000

His rounded face
Filled with graceful ease
Within swaddling layers
Soft gentle edges of
His world enfold him
Also our family
Touching innermost thoughts
When we gaze upon him
Jack Jack we repeat his name
Again again then touch
Soft fingertips almost visible
Along edges of his blanketed world
Parents grandparents great grandparents
Cousins friends neighbors
Gather round our newborn prince
Celebrating his entrance into our lives
We look forward to each
New hour that leads to each
New day as Jack shines
His joy into what will never
Be a mundane world
Since he joined us
In what will soon be
Seven days tomorrow.

NANCY

The Sinatra tune "Nancy With A Smiling Face" comes into my brain often, when I least expect a reminder of a dear friend. I'll be cooking dinner, drifting into the tune, and I call and almost see her face. Her name was Nancy. She lost her smiling face when she learned she had cancers. One cancer would be more than enough for any one of us. Nancy tried to smile some of the time. In time she cried more, smiled less.

She did make many of us smile when she would relate her experiences of her thoughts at Sloan-Kettering. She would make faces into the hospital security cameras, just for the sheer momentary delight. At one Catholic hospital Nancy, a Christian Scientist, slipped into the chapel in her white hospital gown, pulling her IV and holding her outstretched arms for the camera to catch. She believed she did bring a smile or two to those who were bed-bound and bored upstairs. Nancy was impish in the most effective way. She created smiles as a result. Nancy loved her trips to Ireland. Women on a busy bus in Dublin would wink in approval in Nancy's direction, nodding to one another with universal satisfaction.

The most difficult time for those of us who were there with Nancy was to witness her daily decline and her corresponding cynicism. She became more and more negative when she accepted the reality of her condition. Our circle of friends often felt helpless, yet we kept reaching out to Nancy. There were little lulls of despair matched by crescendos of spirited enthusiasm for walks in and around the neighborhood, up and down the main street of Edinboro.

Nancy loved to look for coins on the sidewalk when we walked. We would take turns going with Nancy, each sharing a conversation coupled with whatever merriment we could conjure. It became a contest. We would try to find more money matching Nancy as she scooped up her pennies, dimes and occasional quarters. Nancy had superwoman eyes; she could spot a tarnished coin from far away. There was always a gleam in Nancy's eyes when she put the penny into her pocket. The proceeds from our outings would be set aside for liquid refreshments, usually hot tea in the wintertime, sometimes iced in the warmer months. Nancy's health declined slowly, painfully.

Our friend Nancy was also a world traveler. She had traveled with her family when her son and daughter were young.

Her husband died suddenly, abruptly shocking Nancy since she assumed she would be leaving him alone. His death was just another assault on her already battered psyche. She had envisioned him at her bedside in her final weeks. After his death she fought back with a firm resolution, going on trips abroad with other widows. Even though she seemed weak, Nancy had a strong stubborn streak that propelled her, gave her the inner strength to sign up for yet one more trip. Her last trip was to Istanbul, an apt final resting place for a woman who loved exotic places.

She succumbed to her illness after being transported to a Turkish hospital. No doubt she was surely pleased to finish out her last days in the intriguing metropolis. I like to think she was smiling ever so softly on her last trip.

A decade later, my photos of Nancy smiling, sometimes laughing heartily, sustain me during days devoid of energy and enthusiasm, days that could cause me to cry and curl up in a cold corner of the house. We do inspire one another time and time again. Nancy's friends hold the memory of her courage and our days together. We want her smiling face to appear like the swoop of a magician's wand. I know I will never have her unique and extraordinary presence again. When I find a coin, I realize Nancy's ongoing influence. When I listen to the tune "Nancy" I am reminded of the gift of friendship.

Always alongside us.

RETIREMENT

What I like about retirement is freedom
to walk whenever it seems good to walk
without waiting until after coming home from
work, having every day seem like a weekend,
with days that do not drag yet minutes are a
mere blink, much too rapid, like the
rush of water over Niagara Falls, when we
want to slow down yet cannot because
wide open spaces are meant to be explored
or at least looked at more than once when one
has options that one did not have before
settling into retirement years

PONDERING

"I write because I don't know what I think until I read
what I say."

Flannery O'Connor

Trees heavy with snow
Set the scene
Plenitude produced
Playful pondering
Looking outside
Feeling warm cozy
Gazing upon icy rooftops
Stretched outside my
Writing window.
These are lazy days
When we can take time
To forget what
Matters least
Housebound with
Roads icy
Not conducive to certain
Trips to the lake front
When I walked along the bay
Squishing sand in my toes
Warm thoughts like simmering soup
Penetrate my brain
Leftovers from last summer.

TIME

This is the time when we
Notice each friend's
Gray hair peeking through
Mixed colorations
When friends, parents
Are dying   forcing us
To think of limits to our time
Knowing there were
Important things we wanted
To do but did not do
Because of lack of time
Now we have time to
Read obituaries
We notice wrinkles
When we look into mirrors
Yet know it was our choice
Not to buy Botox
Rather we wanted travel time

Now we wonder that if our parents
Are in the winter of their lives
We are now into our own late autumn
Not ready to face winter storms
Wishing to prolong penetrating
Fragrances when we rake leaves
Inhale hot apple cider
Mulling inside kitchen walls
Not wanting to think about
How cold it can be in wintertime

PALMER SQUARE
Princeton, New Jersey

You took up too many
Rooms in my house
Never gave me room for
My own thoughts,
Time to breathe.
You said, "We do
What we can do."
Here without you
I look ahead
Not tempted to recall
Your skittish eyes
Your squinted face
When I closed
The door then
Turned the key
Knowing I was
Secure once again

NOODLES IN THE KITCHEN

Before the age of pasta machines, when my mom and grand-mother would mix, then hang their homemade noodles to dry on wooden broomstick handles in our kitchen, the long, fine strings of pasta would hang limp as wet socks on the clothes-line. If we walked past the pasta we would quietly take a few strands and proceed to eat them raw. We thought it was adventuresome to eat raw dough. My brothers said it would put hair on their chest, according to our grandparents. My sister and I did not want to be wimpy and not try a taste test, although we did not like the gooey, unsavory aftertaste.

We lived in a modest two-story, green trimmed, white frame house. There were seven of us, including our maternal grandmother living in what then seemed like a large home. We had a spacious wrap-around porch that covered two sides of the house. Years later when we went back to our family home it did look considerably smaller, much more miniscule compared to the largeness of our memory.

Many of the important issues discussed in our family were often debated while we sat around our kitchen table. We had a formal dining room we used for holiday and birthday celebrations. The real questions of the day were settled or at the least presented in our large, looming kitchen. We asked the tough questions: sometimes we would ask permission to go out on date in a car alone with a boy. We would also hear (for us) painful answers: no, you cannot go out on a date in a car alone with a boy. In many ways the kitchen table was our family counterpart to the psychoanalytic couch. Both are hard and flat and both are basic, sturdy workbenches.

We convened at "the" table each weekday evening in order to complete our school assignments. In those days we always had more than one subject to review each day. As the assigned homework increased each successive week, and as we progressed into junior high school (we did not have middle schools), we would then spread out (there were three siblings) onto the dining room table, a natural overflow for our abundant notebooks, books, and pens and pencils. This was before the era of personal computers and cell phones. We had one family telephone that after many years was changed from a multi-party line to a coveted private line. That was a technological leap for our family. I recall if we picked up the phone and another party was talking, etiquette dictated that you immediately and softly replaced the receiver and waited to use the telephone after what was determined a "reasonable" amount of time. Some of the people on the multi-party line were neighbors and our parents reminded us to be kind and thoughtful. We never questioned their telephone rules nor any other parental suggestion.

Each of our parents helped with our homework assignments. My dad was a math whiz and unfortunately that was not one of my best subjects. I preferred to curl up in a corner of a room and read. My tears fell upon my papers at the table as together we worked on my math problems. Fortunately, through the efforts of my dad's tutoring, I managed to meet my math challenge. Eventually I was able to deal effectively with advanced plane geometry and trig. There has been a personal math regression these days. I now use a fast and easy hand calculator or I quickly log on to my computer.

Without my father's faithful math tutoring I would never have succeeded. My dad made a difference. I had top math grades in high school and graduated at the top one percent of my class.

The significance of my parents' influence was that in turn I was able to work with my two sons when they were doing school assignments. Based upon my positive grade school experience, I was well aware of the importance of time and attention as a parent.

And since experience is a formidable teacher, my own family followed the same routine. One of the best places for doing homework in our home was in our kitchen, around our large oak table. I was then able to relive and replay my parents' position by extending my constant commitment to my sons with the same dedicated support. I firmly believe that if more parents would spend evenings sharing and discussing homework and school related assignments, instead of each family member going to their own respective rooms, they could find they could make a difference in their children's lives. Parenting takes a steady commitment to spend time with one another. We still need our personal space, but the best gift we can give to one another is our time.

From my experience, the kitchen table gives the entire family a place to sit down and actually talk to one another within close proximity, eyeball to eyeball. Talking meaningfully to one another is the key. A balance of time, along with kindness and patience, does make a difference. Thinking back to the images of noodles drying in the kitchen, I know I am a product of the kitchen parenting system. As a result, I will continue to advocate the kitchen as one of the most important communication centers in the house; televison, video, and computers be damned (actually given secondary importance). Forget the den, the office, the Great Rooms. Pour some orange juice or make some hot chocolate and invite your family to join you. Try the kitchen as a place to eat, drink, and communicate. Take it from one kitchen graduate, it's worth a try.

A ONE WOMAN'S WORDS

*They sat in the pleasant gloom of later afternoon, staring at each
other through the remains of the party: the silver glasses, the silver
tray, the traces of many perfumes: they sat together watching the
twilight flow through the calm living room that they were leaving
like the clear cold current of a trout stream.*
Zelda Fitzgerald. SAVE ME THE WALTZ

Cold currents conjured up our past,
Former years when we were left with remains,
Empty silver trays, goblets, wine decanters,
Perfumes part of stagnant air,
Disagreeable debris surrounded
Set up a stronghold,
We avoided saying anything since we did not have
Anything to say that could make a difference.
Anxious to close our eyelids and escape,
We went upstairs as quickly as possible,
Never picking up until next day,
When our young son had to tiptoe through
The mess we were living and breathing.

Every life lived in dread
Becomes more dread filled
Each passing day
Except for occasional lull
Never enough to
Heal deep wounds,
Scars securely embedded,
Etched mind filled recollections
We move on, alone,
Determined to seek,
Find another way,
Our way.

HEAD IN THE SAND

Many middle-aged women could write a book
about sweats and chills that come upon them
without warning at inopportune times when
standing in front of an august group giving a
noteworthy speech or when they are about
to be photographed after receiving an award or when
they are gathered for a celebratory dinner and dressed
to the nines or when in jeans and a tee getting groceries
seeing friends including a former colleague who
wonders with his eyes why her flushed face is beet-red.
He further fantasizes she dropped her peaches
because she still has the hots for him but in reality
he is unaware she is more than anxious to
return to the privacy of her home
and kitchen for her Sylvia Plath treatment
when, for a minute of relief from the sweat
she sticks her head into the freezer.

SAVANNAH: 2003

In late June's sweltering high humidity I walked with
Ann and Bea along streets of Savannah admiring
stately southern architecture stretching from street
to street spilling into tree-lined public squares past
benches with an elderly man and woman reading as a
restless baby squirmed in a young woman's arms.

Slowly we walked past homes that oozed Civil War scenes
when slaves wept and swept
front steps before their emancipation
times before the *Garden of Good and Evil* left an imprint
upon modern travelers who want to see inside
Mercer House.

A singing troubadour seemingly smirking disturbed our
riverfront walk; his *Old Gray Mare Ain't What She
Used To* Be innuendoes crashed
pointedly into our ears, splotched conversation, rushed for
cover into sweet smelling candy shops;
all agree we are where we should be this moment sniffing
sugar scents for buoyancy.

In need of respite we reassuringly found
cool comfort in dark corners of a coffee house,
tables piled high with an abundance of current newspapers
sipped our iced coffee taking pleasure in sunken
squeaky floors oversized old sofas and soft oak library
tables lining the periphery
settled into easy chairs with sighs of relief.

Maybe I will return to Savannah, walk again along
winding waterfront yet hope the troublesome troubadour
has traveled to another place. I would not want to hear his
mean melody.

MAGENTA DAYS

An artist was dreaming of a canvas
That was covered with vivid splashes of
Verdant green below a bright mauve tree with
A calico dog whose tail had radiant red spots
Tethered by a leash held by a young girl
She carried a pink parasol with light purple lace
Wear gloves that matched her lemon dress
And rainbow ribbons around collar and cuffs
Complementing her lapis lazuli eyes were
Bright blue boots with shiny silver buckles
All brilliant and splendid on a sunny day
Before thunderclouds roiled overhead
Bringing gray skies to their world.
As the artist grew sad she began to cover
The scene with splotches of burnt sienna
While tree limbs bowed down with weight
Of wind and thunder giving girl and dog
Reason to run for cover before being
Swished into oblivion by brushstrokes on palette.

ACKNOWLEDGMENTS

The late Henri J. M. Nouwen said: "…fear and anxiety never totally leave us. But slowly they lose their domination as a deeper and more central experience begins to present itself. It is the experience of gratitude. Gratitude is the awareness that life in all its manifestations is a gift for which we want to give thanks. What seemed a hindrance proves to be a gift. Thus gratitude becomes a quality of our hearts that allows us to live joyfully and peacefully even though our struggles continue."

I am filled with gratitude for my parents, for their longstanding love, support, and inspiration. In their eighties they continue to fight against the ravages of breast cancer, prostate cancer, and arthritis. Alzheimer's disease now threatens to shake their world. Despite the formidable obstacles caused by the disease, they continue to exhibit courage. Their strong will to live with dignity, intermixed with some semblance of normalcy similar to what they once had, gives poignant testimony to their inner strength. In this the winter of their life journey they are bold, brave travelers. I am blessed because of them.

I am also grateful for the love and support of my immediate family, including Franklin, Heather and family, Jonathan, Valerie, David and John. Each of my siblings, their spouses and families have supported me over the years in the best of ways. I could not have grown and prospered without their constancy. They are a blessing.

I am deeply grateful my son Franklin could design the book cover. Also I value the artwork of my sister Valerie.

Gratitude is also lovingly extended to the circle of friends that include Barbara Tan and Ron Reinig, Annette McElroy, Mel LoPresto, Grace Kerr, Joanne and David

Munzert, Jackie Kitlas, Ebby Conway, Sueann Cook, Linda Carlton, Joseph Montone, Ron Boak, and others living in Edinboro and in Yardley, Pennsylvania. Their gift of time is priceless. I am blessed.

Others writers who have helped to shape and mold my career include Nola Garrett, members of the Mercyhurst College Second Tuesday Poetry Workshop, Diana Hume George, who patiently spent many tutoring hours helping me to see some literary light, and members of the Creative Nonfiction Writers Group of Erie, whose talent and sharp vision enable me to move to new levels of achievement. They are a blessing.

I am grateful for the friendship and good will of the Edinboro University of Pennsylvania family, and particularly President Frank Pogue and his wife Dorothy.

I am also grateful to President William P. Garvey, President, Mercyhurst College, Erie, Pennsylvania for his continued support of the Second Tuesday Poetry-Prose Workshop. We have been meeting for over a decade due to the sponsorship of Dr. Garvey.

I am grateful beyond words to John Edwards for his patient, reliable, and expert editing. Without his keen editing eye I could never achieve a finished manuscript. He is a blessing both as a friend and as talented editor and publisher.

Barbara Grippe was born and raised in Monroeville, near Pittsburgh, Pennsylvania. She was a professor at Edinboro University of Pennsylvania and a member of the Baron-Forness Library Staff.

After an early retirement she was a visiting scholar at Princeton University, Firestone Library, Archives Department, researching the letter collection of F. Scott Fitzgerald. Prior to her retirement, she was a co-coordinator of the Mercyhurst College Community Prose and Poetry Workshop.

She received a Writing Award from Graywolf Press and from the Chautauqua Arts Council. She also received a writer's residency at Hambidge (Georgia) Center for the Arts. Her work has been published by Clarion University of Pennsylvania, Arts Council of Chautauqua, Mercyhurst College, and the *Bucks County Writer*.

Currently she resides in Erie, Pennsylvania.

*

Franklin Grippe received his undergraduate degree in Applied Media Arts from Edinboro University of Pennsylvania. He has practiced professionally for various firms in the visual communications field for the last eight years.

INDEX

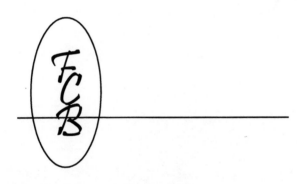

French Creek Books

an Imprint of
Cambridge Springs Press